Frontispiece: Detail from the 'Mosaic Standard' from Ur (BM. 121201), showing a banquet. The original shows, on opposite sides, scenes of 'peace' and 'war'. About 2600 B.C. Height of band *c.* 5 cm.

ANCIENT MUSICAL INSTRUMENTS OF WESTERN ASIA

IN THE DEPARTMENT OF
WESTERN ASIATIC ANTIQUITIES, BRITISH MUSEUM

1.25

Ancient
MUSICAL INSTRUMENTS
of Western Asia

IN THE DEPARTMENT OF
WESTERN ASIATIC ANTIQUITIES,
THE BRITISH MUSEUM

By JOAN RIMMER

LONDON 1969
PUBLISHED BY THE TRUSTEES OF
THE BRITISH MUSEUM

SBN 7141 1045 0

Printed in Great Britain by
Hazell Watson & Viney Ltd,
Aylesbury, Bucks

LIST OF PLATES

6

LIST OF FIGURES IN THE TEXT

7

FOREWORD

It is today more clearly seen than ever before that from very earliest times the Near East, straddling the crossroads of three continents, Asia, Europe and Africa, played a vital part in developing the arts, crafts and sciences of the civilised world of today, indeed was the nursery of most of what the Western hemisphere inherited. In this great phase of development and inventiveness Western Asia shared the lead with Egypt. We are here only concerned with the history of one form of art—Music, and in one of these two areas—Western Asia, extending from Turkey eastwards through Iran to Afghanistan and from the Black Sea southwards to the Red Sea, through Iraq and the coastal states of the Levant as far as South Arabia. The contribution of this area to music suffices on its own for a study, and we are fortunate that the British Museum's Department of Western Asiatic Antiquities is sufficiently rich to illustrate most phases of the story, hitherto never attempted in full. Miss Joan Rimmer has kindly consented to prepare for the Trustees this small book on Ancient Musical Instruments of Western Asia. She has been assisted by Mr. T. C. Mitchell, Assistant Keeper in the Department, who has supplied technical information, contributed some notes and bibliographical references and added two appendices, (i) giving the list of musical instruments illustrated by the Department's collections, and (ii) on music in the Old Testament. The text figures were drawn by Miss M. M. Howard (no. 6) and Miss R. C. Ludovici (nos. 2–5, 7–12).

R. D. BARNETT,

March 1968

Keeper, Department
of Western Asiatic
Antiquities

9

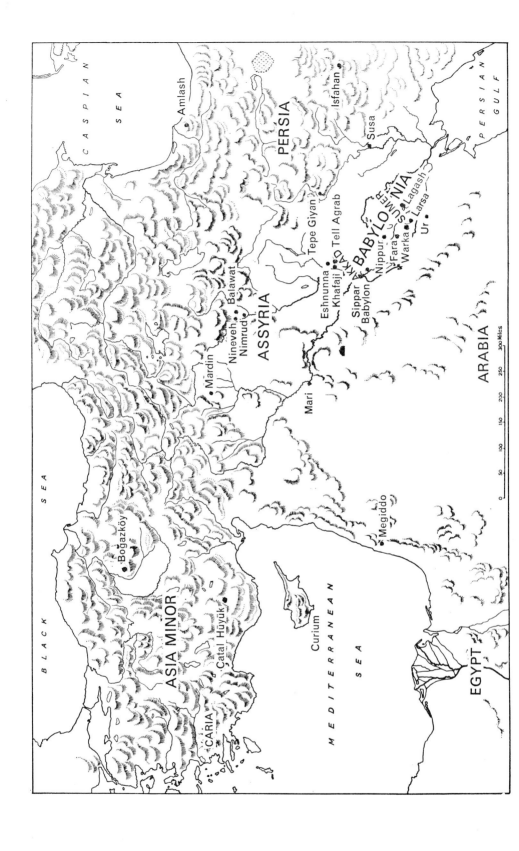

MAIN ARCHAEOLOGICAL PERIODS WITH APPROXIMATE DATES

Early Dynastic period I-III	2800–2370 B.C.
Akkadian period	2370–2110 B.C.
Third Dynasty of Ur	2110–2000 B.C.
Old Babylonian period	2000–1600 B.C.
Kassite period	1600–1100 B.C.
Middle Assyrian period	1350–1000 B.C.
Assyrian Empire period	1000– 612 B.C.
Neo-Babylonian period	612– 539 B.C.
Achaemenid Persian period	539– 330 B.C.
Hellenistic period	330– 250 B.C.
Parthian period	250 B.C.– 230 A.D.

THE musical instruments, both actual and depicted, which are preserved in the Western Asiatic collections of the British Museum are survivals from a long time-span—the third millennium B.C. to the early centuries of the Christian era. To the casual onlooker of the twentieth century, with no thread of tradition or experience to link him with the ancient Near East, the musical activities of those three millennia have little depth or reality. Beautiful, cumbersome, archaic instruments sit mutely behind glass, their music and techniques unrecorded and unknown; musician figures in clay and stone give sometimes a hint about their function but never about their music; written records rarely refer to music and where they do, they are generally ambiguous at best, and often untranslatable.

In at least one respect there must have been a degree of continuity in musical tradition from the Early Dynasties of Sumer to the time of the last Assyrian kings, for the originally Sumerian religious observances and rituals and presumably the function of the music that was an integral part of them, were continued in some form throughout; Babylonians, Kassites and Assyrians were conquerors of men and pillagers of cities, but not destroyers of the gods whose worship they inherited from the Sumerians. Nevertheless, while the musical instruments of the Early Dynasties have associations reaching far back into Neolithic times, those of Assyria at the height of her power and of the later Hellenistic period often have some relation, in form or in the context of use, to instruments which were later developed in European, Asiatic and African societies.

THE THIRD MILLENNIUM IN MESOPOTAMIA

THE lyres, harps and silver pipes which were found in the so-called 'Royal Cemetery' at Ur (to be described below) are the earliest examples we have of musical sound-makers from a highly evolved urban civilisation. However, we know less of the processes of evolution which produced these instruments than of those which produced the civilisation itself. The historian of musical instruments is faced with a considerable gap in physical evidence between the known instruments of the Stone Ages (whistles, whistle and rim-blown flutes, panpipes, rattles, pot drums, scrapers) of which many have survived, and the mature musical artifacts of Bronze Age societies. To some extent, evidence may come from present-day societies at an equivalent stage of development; but none of these is in precisely the situation of Mesopotamia in the fifth and fourth millennia B.C., and it is not always easy or even possible to determine whether an instrument from a present-day society is a survival of an ancient prototype or a retrogression from a later form. It is, however, certain that these 'civilised' Mesopotamian instruments, from which the sound was produced by vibrating animal-gut stretched over a resonator (lyres and harps) and by vibrating cane reeds attached to tubes (double pipes) had evolved during the period following what is generally called 'the Neolithic revolution'. This is the great epoch (about 9000 B.C.–4000 B.C.) when plants were cultivated, cattle domesticated, and most of the crafts of which the products increase human comfort and convenience were first practised.

The keeping of cattle and the raising of crops mean involvement in, and cooperation with, the cycle of Nature. The life and prosperity of the great Sumerian cities were as dependent on reproductive Nature as those of any earlier Neolithic farming community had been, and the festivals of Sumerian religion, though developed far beyond primitive fertility rites, still marked the changing seasons, the greatest festival being the fertility ritual of the New Year. The bull seems already to have been the symbol of fertility in the seventh millennium B.C., to judge by the reliefs of bulls and goddesses in the shrines of Çatal Hüyük in Anatolia.[1] For the Sumerians, it was a symbol associated with a god, and the connec-

1. J. Mellaart, 'Excavations at Çatal Hüyük, 1963, Third Preliminary Report', *Anatolian Studies* XIV (1964), Figs. 7, 9, 14 and Pl. IV.

tion of the unique and characteristic old Sumerian lyre with the bull and whatever he symbolised is evident both from early depictions and from the form and decoration of surviving examples.

LYRES A lyre, in organological classification, is an instrument with open strings which are fixed at the upper end over a yoke held by two arms, and then pass over and parallel to a resonator to which they are finally attached. The term 'lyre' is applied to all instruments of this type, however simple or complex. There seems to be a clear distinction between, on the one hand, the actual lyres of the Early Dynastic III period (Pl. 11) found in the cemetery at Ur—a type excellently depicted on the Ur standard (frontispiece)—and on the other, representations of lyres on cylinder seals of the Early Dynastic II period from Fara,[2] slightly earlier than the Ur burials. The latter, because of their simpler form, suggest representations of archaic, or at least conservative, rather than typical contemporary instruments. Fragments of these seals show fairly small lyres with a sound-box sometimes roughly, or reasonably precisely, in the form of a bull-body profile, sometimes merely rectangular. There are only four strings. The seals are coarsely cut and show no details of string-fixing: the strings appear to emerge directly from the bull-body, suggesting, perhaps, the voice of the god-symbol produced from his own guts. The strings are fixed on a symmetrical plan between sound-box and yoke, either parallel or fan-wise, and these stringing plans appear also in certain representations of the time of Early Dynastic III from Ur itself,[3] Early Dynastic II from Fara[4] and Early Dynastic III from Mari.[5] The asymmetrical stringing on the half of the yoke nearest the player which is characteristic of the later Sumerian lyres must have been dictated by their great size and greater number of strings. It appears to a slight degree in lyres on two seals of Early Dynastic III at Ur[6] (again possibly showing otherwise old-fashioned instruments) which are bull-bodied like the older examples, but are large and have five strings tuned by the same method as some of the big eleven-stringed lyres. But the only known object in two dimensions which might have given a clue about the kind and size of lyre used in religious rituals in the

2. E. Heinrich and W. Andrae, *Fara* (Berlin, 1931), Pls. 64–65.
3. L. Legrain, *Ur Excavations*, III, *Archaic Seal-Impressions* (London, 1936), Pl. 19, no. 372.
4. Heinrich and Andrae, *Fara*, Pl. 65.
5. A. Parrot, *Mari* (Paris, 1953), Pl. 64.
6. C. L. Woolley, *Ur Excavations*, II, *The Royal Cemetery* (London, 1934), Pls. 193, no. 21, 194, no. 22.

middle of the third millennium is unfortunately in a fragmentary state. It is one of two small statues (not in the British Museum) representing Ur-Nanshe, singer of King Iblul-il of Mari. Ur-Nanshe holds what appears to be part of a stringed instrument, no doubt that which she played in rituals in the temple of Ishtar in which the statues were found. But it is unfortunately too broken to discuss.

Of all the lyre-types which may have co-existed during the Early Dynasties of Sumer, it seems certain that the large eleven-stringed instrument was the one used in elegant non-ritual music. This is the lyre played by one of the two musicians on the 'peace face' of the Ur 'standard' (frontispiece). The other figure is a female singer, coiffed and clothed exactly as was Ur-Nanshe. It is interesting that this scene, one of our earliest depictions of music at a princely dinner, can be paralleled again and again during the next four thousand years. The chanting, with a stringed instrument background, of traditional myths of gods and heroes, of epics, praise odes, genealogies and proverbs, has taken place in many Bronze Age societies. It was already an ancient practice when Greek epics sung in Homeric form were committed to writing. It survived into the early Middle Ages in Western Europe, to the end of the sixteenth century in Ireland, and goes on even now in the Balkans, where its practice has been superbly documented by the late Milman Parry.[7]

One of the most astonishing pages in the history of excavation was written when in 1927 Mr. (later Sir) Leonard Woolley, excavating at Ur of the Chaldees on behalf of the British Museum and the University Museum of Pennsylvania, found an amazingly rich Sumerian royal cemetery of the Early Dynastic Period, c. 2500 B.C. In it, forming a special surprise, were the mass burials of scores of courtiers and servants entombed with rich treasure with their king and queen. All this Woolley removed with consummate skill.

Remains of nine lyres were found at Ur; two can be identified with certainty as eleven-stringed lyres. They are from the tomb of Queen Pu-abi (formerly read Shub-ad). Although the basic wooden structure of the silver lyre (Pl. II) had disintegrated, its silver casing, decorative inlay and frontal plaque and bull's head survived, also the silver sheaths of the sticks or levers by means of which the string tension was altered and the instrument tuned. No sticks were used in the rougher and possibly earlier method of string attachment and tuning which was also

7. Milman Parry Collection, Harvard (disk recordings): Milman Parry, A. B. Lord and Bela Bartok, *Serbo-Croatian Heroic Songs* (Harvard, 1954).

used later on some Greek lyres and is still in use in parts of Africa. A narrow strip of cloth or leather is wound round the yoke, the string is then wound to a considerable thickness on top of it so that it grips and holds firmly on the base. The whole roll of foundation and strings is turned in one piece to alter the string tension. The lever method, which is also still used on certain African lyres, appears to be easier to manipulate and more efficient. In this, the string is fixed to a stick (all the silver sheaths have a small perforation through which the string may have been knotted), then wound round yoke and stick in such a way that a pull on the stick tightens or loosens the string. In the lyre shown on the Ur standard (frontispiece) the strings are apparently fixed at the lower end directly into a slanting bridge, presumably knotted as in the modern guitar. No bridge survived with the silver lyre (Pl. II), but its impression remained on the casing of the sound-box, also string impressions which make it appear that the strings were not fastened to the bridge, as in the instrument shown on the Ur standard, but passed over it and were fixed at the bottom of the box. A relief of the time of the Dynasty of Akkad from Lagash, now in the Louvre, shows an interesting lyre, with a bull head at the front of the box and also a complete bull figure standing on it, whose eleven strings appear to be fastened at the bottom of the box in this way. It is possible that the other eleven-stringed silver lyre, of which only the yoke and one arm survived,[8] was tuned by the roll method, for the yoke carries eleven thickish impressions where the strings were fixed and no stick sheaths or sticks were found.

Another, smaller lyre was found in the entrance passage of the tomb of Queen Pu-abi at Ur but of it there remained only the inlaid edging of the sound-box consisting of lapis lazuli, red limestone and shell, the frontal plaque of animals and the lion-headed eagle Im-dugud and the hero Gilgamesh, and the magnificent bull's head of gold and lapis lazuli. The sound-box was probably painted black, for fragments of black-painted wood were found along with the inlay. It was wrongly reconstructed by its discoverer, who did not realise that he had found two instruments, a harp (Fig. 2) and a lyre (Fig. 3), which had collapsed into one.[9]

The curious eight-stringed instrument played by an ass which is shown in the plaque at the front of the gold lyre now in the University

8. Now in the University Museum, Philadelphia, they are at present amalgamated with the remains of a harp.

9. [A paper dealing with these instruments was read by Dr R. D. Barnett at the XVth International Assyriological Congress at Liège in 1966. To appear in *Iraq*, 31 (1969). A fresh reconstruction will be undertaken in due course.]

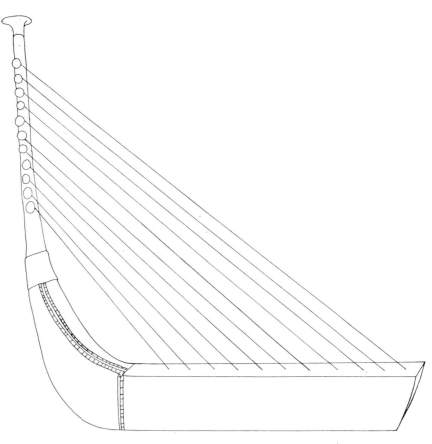

2. Arched harp from Ur, *c.* 2600 B.C. Provisional drawing. Lower part of
the 'harp' of Pu-abi, after projected reconstruction (BM. 121198).

Museum, Philadelphia,[10] seems to have both thick rolls and levers. We
have no means of knowing whether such a combination was indeed used;
binding round the yoke is not needed in the lever method. But the
ass's lyre is a whimsy instrument, perhaps intentionally so, in other
respects. It has symmetrical fan-shaped stringing which is nowhere else
shown on a big lyre, absurd placing of the depression in the upper edge
of the sound-box near the front instead of behind the strings, and recum-
bent instead of standing bull's legs.

The lyres found in the burial chambers at Ur were made of wood,
cased or decorated with gold or silver and embellished with semi-

10. Woolley, *Ur Excavations*, II, Pl. 105.

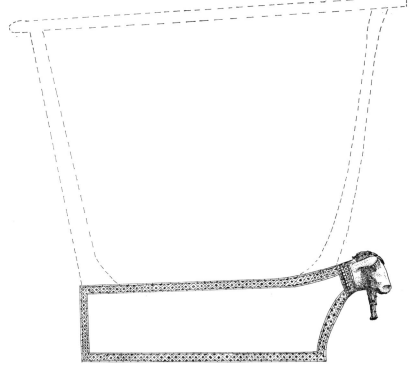

3. Small lyre from Ur, *c.* 2600 B.C. Provisional drawing. Upper part of the 'harp' of Pu-abi, after projected reconstruction (BM. 121198).

precious stones. These are the materials which occur in an enigmatic refrain in the Sumerian composition which tells of Inanna's descent to the nether world. The narrative is punctuated six times by the mournful prayer on behalf of Inanna to different gods (trans. S. N. Kramer):

O Father Nanna, let not thy daughter be put to death in the nether world,
Let not thy good metal be covered with the dust of the nether world,
Let not thy good lapis-lazuli be broken up into the stone of the stoneworker,
Let not thy boxwood be cut up into the wood of the woodworker,
Let not the maid Inanna be put to death in the nether world.

It is possible that this refers to the lyre itself, the instrument which probably accompanied the chanting of the epic, rather in the way that the harp was often referred to by Irish poets who identified person and instrument. We do not know which woods were used for the sound-boxes of Sumerian lyres but the boxwood mentioned in the refrain is a reasonable possibility. Because of its good resonant qualities, it was used during many centuries in Western Europe for woodwind instruments and not abandoned until heavy keywork, which could be firmly attached only to a much harder wood, was introduced.

We have hardly any information about the lyre music of Sumer and Babylon. It is probable that the instrument's strings were of gut or sinew, and we know that they must have been of different thicknesses as they do not differ greatly in length, and that they were plucked with the fingers, not with a plectrum, as were most later lyres. We do not know whether there was any of the complex plucking with one hand and damping with the other as in later lyre techniques; the curved depression in the sound-box just behind the strings suggests that there may have been. The large lyres were certainly what we would call bass instruments and a full scale model of the silver lyre, made in the British Museum's Research Laboratory, gives a rich, somewhat cello-like sound.

We have as little information about the end of the Sumerian lyre as about its beginning: no archaeological evidence for its survival beyond about 1800 B.C. has yet come to light. A Babylonian document of the Kassite period[11] has been convincingly interpreted as the tuning plan of a nine-stringed instrument. However, the fact that the strings designated 'of the front' appear to be the lowest in pitch suggests that the tuning was that of a harp, not of a Sumerian type of lyre. On the reasonable assumption that the 'front' of a bull lyre is the end away from the player which carries the bull's head or animal figure, the lyre's more forward strings are the shortest and highest in pitch, not the largest and deepest. In any case, it is at present impossible to establish what relation the possibly diatonic scale shown in the Babylonian source bears to the tuning of larger instruments of many centuries earlier.

11. M. Duchesne-Guillemin, 'Découverte d'une gamme Babylonienne', *Revue de musicologie* 49 (1963), pp. 3–17; [and see now A. D. Kilmer, 'The Strings of Musical Instruments: their Names, Numbers and Significance' and M. Duchesne-Guillemin, 'Note complémentaire sur la découverte de la gamme babylonienne' in H. G. Güterbock and T. Jacobsen (eds), *Studies in Honor of Benno Landsberger on his Seventy-Fifth Birthday* (Chicago, 1965), pp. 261–268 and 268–272, and Duchesne-Guillemin, 'A l'aube de la théorie musicale: concordance de trois tablettes babyloniennes', *Revue de musicologie* 52 (1966), pp. 147–162; and D. Wulstan, 'The Tuning of the Babylonian Harp', and O. R. Gurney, 'An Old Babylonian Treatise on the Tuning of the Harp', *Iraq*, 30 (1968), pp. 215–228 and 229–232. It appears from these new studies that the Babylonians first used a five note (pentatonic) and later an eight note (heptatonic) scale.]

HARPS In a harp, the plane of the strings is at an angle to, not parallel with, the sound-box, and the strings ascend or descend directly from the box to a string-carrying arm (or neck in European frame-harp terminology). Remains of three harps were found at Ur. Of one, only fifteen copper nails, part of the tuning pins, and a silver binding and the tip of the arm survived. The remains of another harp were also found, along with the lyre fragments already mentioned, in the entrance to the tomb of Pu-abi but were, surprisingly, confused with them by Woolley. They consisted of fragments of the bitumen-covered sound-box, the thin gold and lapis lazuli edging of the belly, a gold cap and sheath from the arm and eleven gold tuning pins. Of the silver-covered harp found in the so-called 'Great Death Pit'[12] along with the remains of three lyres, the silver casing of the sound-box and of part of the arm survived, also five small silver pins of the arm, presumably part of the tuning pins, of which there must originally have been more on a harp of this size. These instruments were elegant examples of the arched harp—a type which, at its simplest, is a development of the musical bow with resonator. It is possible that the arched harp had not the same associations and functions as the big bull lyre. On an early stamp seal found at Ur[13] it is shown in an erotic scene while on a number of the rectangular votive plaques from Khafaji,[14] Tell Agrab[15] and Fara[16] and on a cylinder seal of the Early Dynastic III from Ur[17] it accompanies ritual or festive drinking. The old Indian and Burmese harps (the first of which was plectrum-plucked and the second finger-plucked), were the last big arched harps to survive in art music, but smaller ones still exist in the northern half of Africa and in Afghanistan, their sweet sound giving, perhaps, a hint of the sonority of the big Sumerian harp.

The long *vertical flute* played by a seated figure on a stone cylinder seal of the Akkadian period (BM. 102417) is one of the rare depictions of this kind of instrument from ancient Western Asia. Rim-blown vertical flutes are shown in Egyptian wall-paintings of the Old and Middle Kingdoms, and this type of flute survives in north Africa, the Middle East and the Balkans. It may well have been common in ancient western Asia, though perhaps of too humble association to be depicted often.

12. Now in the University Museum, Philadelphia, amalgamated with the remains of a silver lyre.
13. Legrain, *Ur Excavations*, III, Pl. 50, no. 369.
14. H. Frankfort, *Sculpture of the Third Millennium B.C. from Tell Asmar and Khafājah* (Chicago, 1939) Pl. 107.
15. H. Frankfort, *More Sculpture from the Diyala Region* (Chicago, 1943), Pl. 65.
16. G. Contenau, *Monuments Mesopotamiens* (Paris, 1934), Pl. ixb.
17. Woolley, *Ur Excavations*, II, Pl. 193, no. 18.

Double pipes, of which the Greek *aulos* is a later example, were already in use in Mesopotamia in the third millennium. The silver pipes which were found at Ur and are now in the University Museum, Philadelphia, are discussed, along with the British Museum's many Assyrian depictions of this kind of instrument, on pages 34–36.

THE OLD BABYLONIAN PERIOD

Seton Lloyd has written of the second millennium that 'this . . . period in Mesopotamia is artistically perhaps the least rewarding field of study in that country's early history'.[18] In the field of musical survivals, however, this is not so, for significant musical material is found, fortunately, as often in objects of small artistic merit as in great works of art.

RATTLES The soundmakers and depictions of musicians which survive from the Old Babylonian period, are of a new kind. Whereas those from the third millennium were aristocratic, kingly or priestly, these are more ordinary things of recognisable use. Babies were soothed and amused with rattles in the second millennium as they have presumably been since the beginning of the human race. Many little 'pie-crust' rattles (Pl. IIIb), with tiny pellets inside and perforations for a string or ribbon, have been found. They have a touching home-made look, for the edges are nicked with a knife or fingernail in just the way that a cook nicks a pie-edge today. The charming rattles in the shapes of hen, bear, two-humped camel, pig, tortoise and hedgehog (Pl. IIIa) are more professional-looking pieces, skilfully observed and executed. They have a curious resemblance to the little animal-shaped whistles of another civilisation which had some parallels with the ancient Mesopotamian— that of pre-Hispanic Central America.

HARPS A considerable number of illustrations of musicians survive from this period on terracotta plaques and figurines. They were not objects individually made by a craftsman but were mass-produced from moulds and occur from the time of the Third Dynasty of Ur onwards (c. 2100 B.C.), production reaching its highest level in the Larsa period (c. 1900 B.C.). There are examples in the British Museum of two pieces cast from the same mould. Some plaques have perforations from which they could be hung up, others have devices to enable them to stand. There must have been a popular demand and market of considerable size, whether the objects were used in household devotions, in simple rituals in small shrines or as votive offerings in the great

18. Seton Lloyd, *The Art of the Ancient Near East* (London, 1961), p. 129.

temples, for Babylonian religious organisation was considerably more complex than that of the Sumerians.

It is generally thought that the musicians depicted had formal connections with religious cult ceremonies. While our knowledge of the nature of the ceremonies is slight, it is probable that the instruments shown on the plaques were used in at least some of them. The lyres of earlier Sumer are no longer seen; here are vertical angular harps, horizontal harps played with a plectrum and drums and lutes.

The *vertical harp* (Pl. va) consisted of a large sound-box with a string-arm set at one end at an angle of about sixty-five degrees; the strings seem to have been fixed to the arm with rolls, similar to those in the early Sumerian lyres. It was held in the lap, the string arm horizontal, the box upright in front of the player's chest. The sound-box was greatly larger in relation to the string lengths than that of the old Sumerian arched harp. What seems to be a small vertical angled harp is shown on one votive plaque[19] from Khafaji. It has two registers: in the upper, a musician holds to the chest an instrument with a large box and a perfectly horizontal string arm—apparently the earliest clear depiction of this kind of harp. It is possible that it evolved in the first place from an arched harp held, so to speak, in reverse, with the sound-box up and the string arm down; several stone plaques show instruments which approximate to this. But we really know nothing of the acoustic experiments which must have preceded, or of the musical demands which may have prompted, the evolution or invention of the vertical angled form. A clear depiction on a well-preserved plaque of the Larsa period[20] from Eshnunna, now in the Louvre, shows a large six-stringed instrument, the box apparently covered by a belly, probably of skin, which is lapped over the box to a depth of about three centimetres. The vertical angled harp must have been a generally accepted instrument by the beginning of the second millennium B.C.—an example, of the late second millennium B.C., occurs on a bronze stand from Curium in Cyprus (Fig. 4)—and it lasted in more elaborate form until the seventeenth century A.D. in Persia and Turkey. The Turkish poet Rawānī wrote of the harp in the sixteenth century:

The harp in magic craft is of great worth
It brings the new moon down from heaven to earth.

Ewliyā Chelebi in the seventeenth century considered that it had been invented by Pythagoras to solace Solomon and wrote:

19. M. L. and H. Erlenmeyer, *Orientalia* 26 (1957), Pl. XVI.
20. E. Strommenger and M. Hirmer, *The Art of Mesopotamia* (London, 1964), Pl. 143.

21

It is a great instrument in the form of an elephant's trunk. It has forty strings and its sound is astonishing. There are but few who play it because it is a difficult instrument.[21]

LUTES   While it is likely that the sound-producing principle of the lute was known in very ancient times, pictorial evidence for it does not appear until the Akkad period in the latter part of the third millennium B.C. (Pl. IVc). A lute consists of a small number of strings stretched

4. Side of a bronze openwork stand showing a seated harpist facing a pillar. From Curium, Cyprus, 12th–11th century B.C. Height 12.5 cm (BM., Department of Greek and Roman Antiquities, 1920–12–20, 1).

across a resonator, as in a lyre, and then along a neck against which they are 'stopped' by the fingers of one hand in order to give notes of different pitch, while the other strikes them over the resonator. This principle is that of the major stringed instruments of Western European civilisation. In the ancient Near East, the open-stringed harps and lyres were more important, and it is likely that the origins of the lute lie, not with the civilised peoples of Mesopotamia, but with barbarian mountain peoples to the northeast of them.

The harp players are solemn, formal, female figures, fully draped

21. Ewliyā Chelebī, *Siyāḥat nāma*, translated and edited by H. G. Farmer in *Turkish Instruments of Music in the Seventeenth Century* (Glasgow, 1937), p. 32.

from neck to ankles. The lute-playing figures are male, sometimes nude, bearded (Pl. ivb) or with long, plaited, barbaric hair styles. Some are shown with animals. On a plaque from Nippur,[22] now in the University Museum, Philadelphia, there is a nude, seated lute-player with a sheep and a barking dog; and a Babylonian boundary stone from Susa, now in the Louvre, shows bearded figures with bows slung at their backs, playing lutes, surrounded by lion, antelope, sheep, ox, horse, panther and ostrich;[23] while on a seal of the Kassite period (c. 1600) two figures with lute and small rectangular lyre appear with antelope, scorpion, monkey and bird.[24] The stiff kilted lute-player standing beside a footed jar (Pl. iva) has no obvious magical or pastoral associations. The seated lute player on the seal of the Akkadian period (Pl. ivc) is playing during a ritual, and the nude lute-playing figure (Pl. ivb) may have some magical significance. No ancient Western Asiatic lutes have survived. However, this early form of lute, with small oval resonator, pole-like neck and two or three strings plucked with a plectrum, was introduced into Egypt by the time of the Middle Kingdom and still exists in North Africa. But today often the resonator is a tortoiseshell covered with camel-skin, the strings are of green nylon, and the neck is brightly and touristically decorated with incised and painted geometric patterns.

DRUMS AND TAMBOURS Considerable numbers of figurines and plaquettes of women holding flat circular objects have been found (Pls. via-c). There is variety in details. Some women wear only girdles or aprons, some also have shoulder decoration (perhaps tattoo marks); some have flattish head-dresses, some wear three-pointed crowns; some hold the circular object below the breasts, some over them; some are exaggeratedly, some merely pleasantly, fat. Most wear one or more heavy necklaces with a large, barrel-shaped, sideways-hung pendant at the centre. These figures have generally been interpreted as being connected with the cult of the Mother Goddess, and the circular objects as being either votive disks or *tambours*, which were almost exclusively women's instruments even in Greek and Roman times. There are a few examples in which an indisputable tambour is realistically represented, held to one side and actually beaten.[25] It seems probable

22. L. Legrain, *Terracottas from Nippur* (Philadelphia, 1930), Fig. 94.
23. *Encyclopédie photographique de l'art*, Louvre, I, p. 267.
24. L. Delaporte, *Musée du Louvre, Catalogue des cylindres* (Paris, 1920), Pl. 51, no. 22.
25. A. Parrot. *Tello* (Paris, 1948), Fig. 49b; and several figurines from Nippur now in the University Museum, Philadelphia.

that the tambour, whether used to mark the rhythm of chanting or dancing or both, would have been played by skilled, professional priestesses or cult leaders. The talent for precise and authoritative performance on drums of any kind is not common, though it is, and perhaps always was, commoner in non-European than in European and European-derived civilisations.

Two fragments in the British Museum's collection of terracottas are of a different character. One is the upper half of a rough figure with very broad shoulders and small head, no head-dress or crown, and hair parted in the middle with big coils over the ears (Pl. vib). It holds a large, deep 'tambour' and apart from the coiled hair it has a curiously masculine look. The other is the upper half of a plaque showing a delicate, slender, draped figure, with flat head-dress and long ringlets, who holds a small 'tambour' or votive disk to its flat chest (Pl. vic). The plaques and figurines date from the second millennium B.C., and we have no certain knowledge of the significance of the different types. There exist, however, dating from the late third millennium, individually shaped figurines without the circular object but wearing the heavy necklaces and girdles of the later examples.[26]

The small terracotta figure of a monkey (Pl. vid) from Babylon, of the seventh or sixth century B.C., is worn to a degree which makes certain identification difficult. He holds over his left shoulder a short, heavy club while his right hand grasps what appears to be the stick of a *friction drum*. This curious instrument, whose origin is generally thought to be connected with neolithic fertility rituals and which survives in Europe today only as a fiesta and fair-ground noise-maker, consists generally of a pot or bowl covered with a skin head, pierced by a stick. When the stick is rubbed with the hand the instrument gives a deep, grunting sound. Though representations of monkeys often appear in religious scenes we do not know their significance.

DANCE AND GAMES Western Christian religion has purposefully excluded physical activity, other than sober processional movement, from its rituals. In most other religions it was and is a natural part of human behaviour towards the Gods. The games and sung dances of the Greeks, the athletic displays of the Celts, were in honour of the Gods; American Indians dance, sometimes for days on end, to ask or give thanks for good crops, or health, or desired wives or husbands; American

26. C. Zervos, *L'art de la Mésopotamie* (Paris, 1935,) pp. 157 and 174; and *Encyclopédie photographique de l'art*, Louvre, I, p. 221, Fig. B.

negro Christian congregations ecstatically sway and clap to complex rhythms. The scene depicted on a terracotta plaque of the early second millennium from Larsa, showing two men wrestling or exercising to the sound of a large, footed drum and *cymbals* (Pl. vb), is possibly of a sacred if athletic nature. There are vividly portrayed wrestling scenes on votive plaques,[27] now in the Iraq Museum, which are at least five hundred years older than this example, and there still remains in Iran and parts of Iraq a tradition of ritual exercise. In the *zurkhane* (house of force) groups of men engage in strenuous and specialised gymnastic exercises directed by a drummer who sometimes also chants extracts from the *Shahnameh* (Book of Kings) of Firdousi; the stages of the exercise are punctuated with cymbals. Though in cities it can be something of a commercial performance, in small communities it is done only at dawn and sunset. The origins of this practice are said to be pre-Islamic and of a partly chivalrous, partly religious character. The small cymbals played on our plaque by the seated female figure (Pl. vb) have a familiar look even in the twentieth century, for they seem to be of the shallow, vertically clashed kind which came into Europe from Turkish sources in the Middle Ages, and which is still a usual component of Western bands and orchestras. No actual cymbals survive from early Mesopotamia in the second millennium, but examples dating from the late second millennium B.C. are known from Palestine.[28]

The large, goblet-shaped *drum* is one of the few ancient Mesopotamian instruments to which a contemporary name (Akkadian *lilissu*) can be attached with reasonable certainty. A late Babylonian text described its body as being of bronze, and it must have had a deep, kettledrum-like sound, solemn and awe-inspiring in the great rituals of the yearly cycle and the cult-ceremonies in which it was used. In Western Europe, percussion instruments have always figured less, both in variety and in usage, than other kinds of instruments—a long-lasting result, perhaps, of the early western Christian church's fear of their hypnotic effect and non-Christian association. To experience today the power and quality of skilled ritual and ceremonial drumming one must turn to Asia, Africa and the Americas.

Some hints of musical activities other than those formally connected with religion occur in texts of this period. For example, among the vast quantities of correspondence in the Royal Archives of Mari is a

27. Strommenger and Hirmer, *Art of Mesopotamia*, Pl. 46.
28. R. W. Hamilton, 'Excavations at Tell Abu Hawām', *Quarterly of the Department of Antiquities of Palestine*, IV (1935), p. 60, no. 369.

letter[29] from Shamshi-Adad (1813–1781) to his son, suggesting that the daughters of Yahdun-Lim be sent to the palace at Shubat-Enlil to be taught singing. We cannot tell whether this was simply to acquire an accomplishment appropriate to high-born ladies or to learn one of the crafts essential to high-born ladies who were to become priestesses. In another letter,[30] Shamshi-Adad orders the killing of members of the Wilanum tribe and arranges the disposal of their women, among whom were two female singers. Two other letters[31] seem to imply that military music, so well documented in Assyrian reliefs of a thousand years later, already existed in some form, for the writer wishes to have apprehended and bound, along with two others, one Sin-iqisham, the singer accompanying the army.

IRAN AND ANATOLIA

Since more is known of the activities of central areas of civilisation than of peripheral areas and surrounding peoples, we have very little knowledge of social background to explain musical materials of the second

5. Fragment of a bronze situla showing a procession of musicians. From Tepe Giyan. See Pl. viib (BM. 128620).

millennium from Iran and Anatolia. It is not possible to identify the scene shown on the fragment of a bronze situla from Tepe Giyan, near Nihavand (west Iran), in which there are two seated and four standing figures (Fig. 5 and Pl. viib), two of which are playing instruments and

29. G. Dossin, *Archives Royales de Mari*, I, *Correspondance de Šamši-Addu* (Paris, 1950), No. 64.
30. Idem., No. 8.
31. Idem., No. 12, and C. F. Jean, *A.R.M.*, II, *Lettres diverses* (1950), No. 4.

two clapping. The second instrumentalist plays a small *rectangular frame drum*. This type, whose most familiar present-day representative is the *adufe* of Spain and Spanish America, was also used in New Kingdom Egypt, in a form with more concave sides. It is not depicted at all in Mesopotamia. The other instrument is somewhat ambiguously depicted. It has been considered an elongated quadrangular harp. Small quadrangular harps are depicted on a few Christian monuments and manuscripts of the tenth to twelfth centuries A.D.,[32] and the Sutton Hoo fragments, of the seventh century A.D.,[33] seem to be the remains of a quadrangular harp. No comparable instrument is at present known from any ancient Western Asiatic source, and the instrument shown here is, more probably, of the *zither* type, shown, not in its flat playing position but upright, as instruments of this kind, including the European medieval psalteries, have always been shown in non-perspective styles of representation. The instrument is more or less rectangular, and both hands are over the strings on the same side, which is the technique of zithers, not of lyres or harps. The left hand is clumsily put below the right, as if by an afterthought of attempted accuracy even farther beyond the artist's technique than was the delineation of the left hands of the clapping figures, which also have defects of perspective. It is interesting that the first Chinese reference to the long zither dates from the end of the second millennium B.C.

The cylinder seal of yellow stone, showing a seated figure with an oversized *lyre* surrounded by files of birds and animals (Fig. 6 and Pl. VIIIa) is said to have been found at Mardin in southeast Turkey. Although the fruits of Mesopotamian civilisation were introduced into Anatolia early in the second millennium by Assyrian merchants, influence from Mesopotamia was only one of many that affected Anatolia, with its extensive Mediterranean and Black Sea coasts. There are many questions about the origin and dispersal of round-based lyres which are as yet unanswered. It is difficult to say whether the instrument shown on the seal was derived from a Cretan source, or whether the similar round-based lyres with a double curve on the arms, which were used in the Minoan and Mycenaean cultures, were derived from those brought to the eastern Mediterranean by peoples who migrated there from Asia Minor early in the second millennium B.C. The most famous example is that played by a dark-skinned woman in a libation scene on a sar-

32. Joan Rimmer, *The Irish Harp* (Dublin, 1968), Pl. 8, Chapter III.
33. Now in the Department of British and Medieval Antiquities of the British Museum.

cophagus from Haghia Triada, now in the Hiraklion Museum, and there are other examples from Palaikastro in eastern Crete and from Pylos in the Peloponnese. These lyres were always shown in a vertical position. The horizontal playing position seems to have been developed on asymmetrical lyres of western Semitic origin, and it is possible that

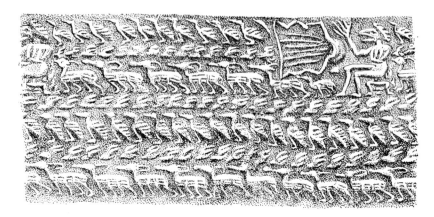

6. Cylinder seal showing a lyre player. From Mardin, southeast Turkey. See Pl. v111a (BM. 134306).

the sideways position here and on other Anatolian seals with similar scenes was adopted for reasons of design rather than accuracy. Although we do not know the significance of these scenes of lyre-players surrounded by birds and beasts, it is tempting to see in them an early form of the Orpheus myth.[34]

The remarkable bronze figurine, of the eighth century B.C., of a piper wearing a scalloped tunic and a Phrygian cap (Pl. viiic) provides a unique depiction of an instrument whose type is still known, in various forms, from the Atlantic coasts of Europe and north Africa to the Urals and India.[35] Like the lyre on the stone cylinder seal, it also provides a link with Minoan Crete, where the first known depiction of a related instrument occurs on the already-mentioned sarcophagus from Haghia Triada. The nature of the reed instruments of the ancient world is discussed more fully on pages 34–36 in connection with the double pipes of Mesopotamian and Assyrian provenance. In brief, the Haghia Triada

34. [Compare the similar scenes of a lyre player with animals on a late second millennium B.C. cylinder seal from Tarsus, and on a painted Philistine flask from Megiddo, T. Dothan, *The Philistines and their Material Culture* [in Hebrew] (Jerusalem, 1967), p. 132 and Fig. 25 (p. 121).]

35. Anthony Baines, *Bagpipes* (Oxford, 1960), pp. 27–68.

pipes and the instrument played by the Anatolian bronze figure are both forms of *hornpipe*—that is, a tube or two parallel tubes with fingerholes, sounded by means of single reeds (vibrating tongues cut, in the simplest form, from the body of the tube itself, but generally from a separate short tube inserted into the upper end of the pipe) and with an upturned horn bell or twin bells at the lower end. The Cretan pipes are long and have a horn attached to the end of one pipe only. It is difficult to say whether those played by this bronze figure are single or double pipes. The thickness of the instrument suggests they are double pipes of identical tuning, with a single horn bell, and the player's hands are carefully shown fingering across both pipes at once—the technique used on existing pipes of this kind. Both single and double pipes exist, however, in mouthblown and bagged forms, and the instrument could equally be a thickly-modelled single hornpipe.

The terracotta figure of about 800 B.C. from Iran, showing a seated man with feline ears or mask (Pl. VIIId), has a *whistle* in his left leg. The whistle head was made separately and then attached to the rest of the figure. We know nothing of the use of such sound-makers in Iran of the eighth century B.C. Clay whistles in human and animal form are still made in Lithuania, Latvia and some of the Volga and trans-Caucasian regions of the Soviet Union. While they are now little more than toys, they may, like the friction drum, originally have been formal sound-makers in fertility ceremonials.

The early history of *trumpets* is generally discussed in terms of the well-documented Egyptian instrument, whose slender tube and flaring bell are familiar from many frescoes and some surviving examples,[36] and the Greek *salpinx*, for which we have no specimens, but a number of literary references and a few pictures. The Greeks sometimes called the *salpinx* 'Tyrrhenian', that is, Etruscan. This attribution makes sense on the assumption of a Lydian or Anatolian origin for the Etruscan people, for there are Anatolian bronze figures of trumpeters, such as that from Caria (Pl. VIIIb) dating from the early Iron Age. But this kind of trumpet, with a thick tube with an incorporated mouthpiece and only slightly flaring bell was already ancient. It must have been used in Mesopotamia at least from Early Dynastic times, for a limestone fragment from Khafaji (now in the Oriental Institute, Chicago), which is apparently part of a victory stela (Fig. 7) has one figure blowing a similar instrument.

36. H. Hickmann, *La trompette dans l'Égypte ancienne* (Cairo, 1946), Supplément aux Annales du Service des antiquités de l'Égypte, Cahier No. 1.

7. Limestone fragment showing a trumpeter, from Khafaji, *c.* 2600 B.C. H. Frankfort, *Sculpture of the Third Millennium B.C. from Tell Asmar and Khafājah* (Chicago, 1939), pl. 110 C (Chicago, Oriental Institute Museum, A. 9273).

ASSYRIA

The series of reliefs in stone and bronze which adorned interior walls and gates of the palaces of the later Assyrian Kings of the 9th–7th centuries B.C. provides a rich and precise source of information about many aspects of the life of the Assyrians and neighbouring peoples. Here are few gods, religious symbols and cult ceremonies but in the main straightforward records of the campaigns, conquests (no doubt exaggerated), triumphs and hunting expeditions of Ashurnasirpal II (883–859 B.C.) who moved the capital from Assur to Kalhu (Nimrud) and his son, Shalmaneser III (859–824 B.C.), Sargon II (722–705 B.C.) who created Khorsabad as his capital, Sennacherib (705–681 B.C.) and Ashurbanipal (668–626 B.C.) who rebuilt the palaces at Nineveh. The subjects of the reliefs are so exactly observed and so competently executed that they give us details of food, clothing, armour, weapons, musical instruments, landscapes, buildings, transport and methods of warfare to a degree which is largely lacking for earlier times. The great value of these reliefs lies in the fact that we get, for the first time, a picture of non-religious as well as religious musical practice in an ancient Western Asiatic society.

It is unlikely that this practice was altogether peculiar to the Assyrians, for cultures were far from self-contained. The instrument apparently most generally used, at least in public music, was an *horizontal angled harp* sounded with a plectrum (Pls. IX, XIII). The plectrum-struck variety of any stringed instrument has always a brighter and more energetic and carrying sound than the finger-plucked variety—a familiar example is the plectrum guitar, even without amplification—and the undoubtedly brisk sonority of a plectrum-struck harp seems to accord well with the thrusting and aggressive character of the Late Assyrian kingdoms. It was not a new instrument; it is depicted on cylinder seals of the early third millennium B.C.[37] and on a plaque from Nippur,[38] and presumably it had superseded the older, plectrum-sounded arched harp, of which a few depictions survive. The Assyrian horizontal harps are curiously elegant, with their long, slim sound-boxes, string-carriers made in the form of a human arm with a delicately carved hand at the end, and eight or nine strings wound round the arm, their tasselled ends falling in a cluster below the sound-box. They were slung from the player's neck—the sling can be seen clearly in Pl. IX—and the technique was probably a compound of damping with the left hand the strings not required to sound, while drawing the slender plectrum over all the strings with the right hand. (This technique of obliterating unrequired notes rather than selecting required ones is used on a modern zither-family instrument, the auto-harp.) The romantic sound, somewhat lush repertoire and unincisive playing generally associated to us in the West with the European pedal harp give us no idea of more vigorous styles of harping. However, the lusty, even martial character of the traditional music played on small horizontal harps by the people of the Abkhaz and Ossetian regions of the U.S.S.R.—both slightly beyond the lands of Assyria's old enemy, the kingdom of Urartu—may represent a peripheral survival of the ancient style, for it is an often-recurring irony in history that some characteristic practices of powerful civilisations continue vigorously among once despised or conquered people long after the civilisations themselves have perished.

Pairs of horizontal harps provide music for animal sacrifices and libation rituals. On the bronze gates of Balawat, which show scenes from the campaigns of Shalmaneser III, one bearded and one unbearded musician play as beasts are led to the place of sacrifice (BM. 124662). A fragment of a stone relief from the Palace of Sennacherib at Nineveh has two bearded and two unbearded harpists. Only bearded musicians, however, play during the pouring of libations over the quarry of hunting expeditions. Stone reliefs from Nimrud (BM. 124533, 124535) and Nineveh (BM. 124886) show Ashurnasirpal pouring libations over a dead bull and a dead lion and Ashurbanipal over dead lions, to the playing of

37. Delaporte, *Louvre, Catalogue des cylindres*, Pl. 32, no. 7.
38. Strommenger and Hirmer, *Art of Mesopotamia*, Pl. 143.

two bearded harpists. In scenes of war and conquest, *frame drums* or *tambours* are added. Another relief from Nimrud, with scenes of Ashur-nasirpal's victorious return from a campaign, shows standard bearers in chariots and soldiers and miming figures taking part in a triumph to music played by two bearded harpists and an unbearded tambourist, whose instrument is slung from the shoulder like the harps (Pl. IX). A bronze relief from Balawat shows lines of bound captives being herded along, followed by two unbearded tambourists who hold their instruments high, and two bearded harpists (BM. 124690).

The *vertical harp* (Pls. X, XII, XIII) differs from that depicted on plaques of the second millennium in being larger overall, in having a sound-box more sharply angled from the string-carrying arm, and more strings, probably about eighteen in all; in Pl. X fourteen are visible and a few more are obscured by the player's body. The belly is lapped over the box, as in the earlier harps, and is fixed to it with closely set studs. Sound holes in the box are shown clearly. The playing position, with the box resting against the left shoulder and the string-arm supported by the right hand or wrist, is consistent in all these reliefs, with the exception of the second figure (incorrectly restored) in Pl. XIII and the technique can be seen in Pls. X and XII. The little finger of the right hand appears to steady the string-carrying arm, the remaining three fingers and thumb being used to pluck the strings close to their fixing-point on the string arm; the player's left arm is more manœuvrable and plucks the strings higher up. This harp presumably had the largest pitch-range of any ancient Western Asiatic instrument. Although its sound, being produced by finger, not plectrum plucking, may have been small compared with that of the horizontal harps, its range of effects would certainly have been greater if the variety of dynamic change and accentuation which is possible on finger-plucked instruments was exploited to any degree. We have no notion of what music the Assyrians played on their vertical harps. But, on the evidence of these reliefs, one tonal subtlety must have been present. A harp-string gives a different quality of sound according to the point at which it is struck—richer and more definite near the sound-box, thinner and more diffused as the distance from the box increases. The notes played by the Assyrian harpist's right hand, moored, as it seems to have been, close to the string-arm and plucking the strings at the furthest point from the box, must have been of a different quality of sound, as well as fewer in number, than those played by his left hand, which was not only free to move over the whole range of strings, but also to strike them nearer the middle. (Striking near the box, the most sonorous point of all, was obviously ruled out on a vertical harp on grounds of non-practicality.) It seems possible that, whatever the music was, it was cast in the texture of one prominent and fairly mobile handful and one subsidiary and less mobile handful. This is, of course, the texture of much double-pipe music also—polyphony in its true sense of 'several soundingness', not in its narrow European sense of written part music.

8. Detail from a bas relief showing a lyre player. From the palace of Ashurbanipal (668–626 B.C.) at Nineveh. See Pl. xv (BM. 118916).

In any society, non-ritual music tends to be more varied and enterprising than ritual music, and it is not surprising to find that the big vertical harp, of greater range and probably of greater expressiveness than any of its contemporary lyres or horizontal harps, should appear in non-religious contexts like the garden scene with a tame lion (Pl. xv) of which Fig. 8 shows a detail, and the feast of Ashurbanipal and his queen in the royal garden (Pl. x). A long drum plays with the harp in this last scene, where, in the idyllic atmosphere of palm- and vine-shaded quiet, with only the sound of birds, fly-whisks and gentle music to stir the air, the modern mind at least is jolted by the severed head of Teumman, the king of Elam defeated by Ashurbanipal, hanging from a tree. One may perhaps remember here the association of the old vertical arched harp with drinking rituals and festive scenes, and also the rather frivolous character which the Greeks attributed to harp music, for them Asiatic and exotic.

All the *lyres* which appear in the Assyrian reliefs are held more or less horizontally and are played with a plectrum. The lyre in Pl. xii, with

33

incoiled, unequal arms and a slightly curved yoke, is of a type which was possibly of Phoenician or Syrian origin, eventually used over a wide area. Depictions of comparable instruments have come from Cyprus[39] and, with a straight instead of a curved yoke, from Megiddo.[40] The three figures followed by an Assyrian soldier in the relief in Pl. xi have been perhaps rather rashly considered by some scholars to be Jewish captives, playing presumably Jewish lyres. One may remember the lament in Psalm 137, 'They that carried us away captive required of us a song'. Others do not identify the figures as Jewish and consider the lyres to be of a kind which was introduced into Assyria in the first half of the second millennium, but was certainly Western or Levantine. There are only a few lyres of this kind known as yet, and the chronology and classification of the many lyre-forms which co-existed in the Near East in the first millennium is neither complete nor certain.

The chronology and classification of the *double pipes* of the ancient world is even less complete and certain. There has been hardly any research on the most familiar form, the Greek *aulos*, and a thorough study of earlier and non-Greek double pipes has yet to be made. No doubt this is largely because practical research can be done only by a competent wind-instrument player who is also expert at experimental reed-making—a combination of talents which is not often found in professional musicians and archaeologists. Another stumbling block has been the long-lasting misconception of the nature of the instruments. This is due to centuries' long misuse of the term 'flutes' in all European languages.

The double pipes of the ancient world, in all their varieties of long and short, parallel and divergent, equal and unequal, straight or bell-ended, were reed instruments; this means that, whatever the material of the tubes, which could be cane, bamboo, metal, wood, ivory or bone, they were sounded by the vibration of a blade or blades of thinned cane —'reeds'—which the player activated with his breath. The tubes were cylindrical (though some Etruscan and Roman pipes made of naturally thick materials such as bone, had slightly conical exteriors) and acoustically the instruments were of the clarinet genus, as are all surviving instruments of the type. The pitch of a cylindrical pipe sounded with a reed is considerably lower than that of conical pipes of the same length, however sounded, and of cylindrical pipes sounded by other means. Even

39. E. Gjerstad, *Opuscula Archaeologica*, IV, *Decorated Metal Bowls from Cyprus* (Lund, 1946), Pls. i, ii.

40. H. T. Bossert, *Altsyrien* (Tübingen, 1951), No. 1161 and G. Loud, *The Meggiddo Ivories* (Chicago, 1939), Pl. 4, no. 2.

the short pipes of the ancient world, no longer than our tin whistles, would have had a medium pitch. The sound, too, is surprisingly rich and resonant, as modern experiments have shown.[41] The difference between sounding with single reeds and with double reeds, often mistakenly taken to be a distinction of instrumental type and sound, with the former making 'clarinet' and the latter 'oboe', is in fact only a difference of degree within the clarinet type, for the basic acoustic behaviour of a reed instrument depends on the shape of its bore, not the single or double nature of its reed. Mouth-blown double reeds, such as were used on the Greek and Roman double pipes and on some earlier pipes, are controllable in dynamic level and nuance to some degree, as can be heard from the cylindrical pipes with long double reeds which still survive in certain regions of Asia. Single reeds, like those used in present-day Mediterranean pipes (which are generally parallel, apart from the divergent triple-pipe *launedda* of Sardinia) and on some ancient double pipes like those described on page 29 are not controllable in this way. They either sound or they do not, and the complexity and subtlety of music played on them is made up from other musical ingredients.

Compared with lyres and harps, there are few depictions of double pipes surviving from Mesopotamia before the Hellenistic period. Among the ritual scenes on the stela of Ur-Nammu (now in the University Museum, Philadelphia) is one in which a bull and lamb are sacrificed. A figure in the background plays long, divergent double pipes which seem to be unequal, though the fragmentary state of the relief makes this less than absolutely certain. The double pipes in the Assyrian reliefs (Pls. XII, XIII) are short and possibly equal in length, though this is again hard to determine exactly because of the poor condition of the stone in Pl. XIII and the crowding of the figures in Pl. XII. Though many equal pipes, both parallel and divergent, were identical, equality of length does not necessarily imply identical tuning in each pipe. The silver pipes (also in the University Museum, Philadelphia) which were found in a badly damaged state in the 'Royal Cemetery' at Ur (Fig. 9), were almost certainly of equal length but are not the same in tuning; one has four finger-holes while the other has only one. We have little evidence as to whether the double pipes of antiquity were or were not overblown into the second register (twelve notes higher than the first, not eight, as with flutes and with reed instruments of conical bore). Assuming that

41. J. A. MacGillivray, *The Cylindrical Reed Pipe; its Classification and Scope*, in *Music, Libraries and Instruments* (London, 1961).

they were not, this assemblage of finger-holes gives an instrument consisting of one melody-playing pipe giving five notes, and a drone pipe with a one-note change, probably five notes higher than the first. The upper ends of the silver pipes are damaged so we do not know their

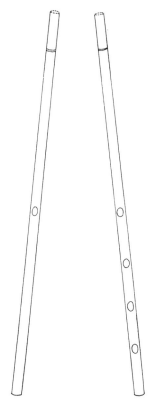

9. Silver pipes from Ur, *c.* 2600 B.C. Reconstruction. See Woolley, *Royal Cemetery* pp. 258–259 (Philadelphia, University Museum, CBS. 17554).

original length, but they may have been only a trifle longer than they are now, which is about twenty-three centimetres. With the additional length of the reeds, this would be more or less the size of the short divergent pipes shown in the Assyrian reliefs, and also approximately that of the pipes shown on a small marble figure from Keros in the Cyclades which dates from the third millennium.

The Elamite musicians in Pls. XIII–XIV comprise seven players of vertical harps, one horizontal harp (inaccurately restored), two sets of divergent double pipes and a small drum, followed by clapping figures, presumably dancers, and one particularly interesting figure, fourth from the right in the back row (Pl. xivb). It has been suggested that this singer is engaged in the performance of wordless *vocalise* heightened by gentle beating on the throat with the right hand in order to give a slow tremolo. This was still done in recent times by certain singers in Turkestan and it is said to produce a most pathetic effect. One can well imagine its suitability on the occasion of submission to the Assyrian king who had conquered and devastated Elam.

The Assyrian reliefs in which *trumpets* are shown are in very poor condition and details of the instruments cannot be seen clearly. The trumpet in Pl. xvi seems to be slightly longer than that in the limestone fragment of Early Dynastic times (Fig. 7). In the bull-hauling scene in Fig. 10, the efforts of the large number of men hauling the great statue which is fixed on a wooden sleigh are synchronised by signals from trumpeters standing on top of the stone figure. It must have been an exhausting blow for the trumpeters as well as an exhausting haul for the labourers, for the reliefs show two figures, one blowing, the other holding his instrument and presumably waiting to take over when the first trumpeter stops.

In hunting scenes, royal horses and those of members of the royal suite who are close to the king generally have *bells* at their necks. While bells may have had, even for the Assyrians, some of the ancient universal association of defence against evil spirits, it is likely that in the hurly-burly of the hunt they had primarily an identifying function. The mount of a horseman in a fragment from Nimrud of the time of Tiglath-pileser III (745–727 B.C.) wears a sizeable cone-shaped bell (Pl. xvii). In the series of reliefs showing Ashurbanipal's hunting exploits, the bells are elongated globular in shape. In the lion-hunt the royal horse's collar, from which the bell hangs, is decorated with floral patterns; the mounts of two horsemen and two archers of the royal suite wear undecorated collars carrying identical bells. In the onager hunt, the same kind of bell is worn by the king's horse, on a collar of different decoration from that in the lion hunt. The horses of his two immediate attendants, an archer and a lance-thrower, wear plain collars with bells which are slightly smaller but the same shape. This relief is in good condition and the turned rim of the royal horse bell can be seen clearly (Pl. xviii).

Of the British Museum's hundred or so bronze bells which have been recovered from Nimrud and other sites, only five are of the size and shape of the royal horse bells in Ashurbanipal's hunts. Pl. xixa shows one

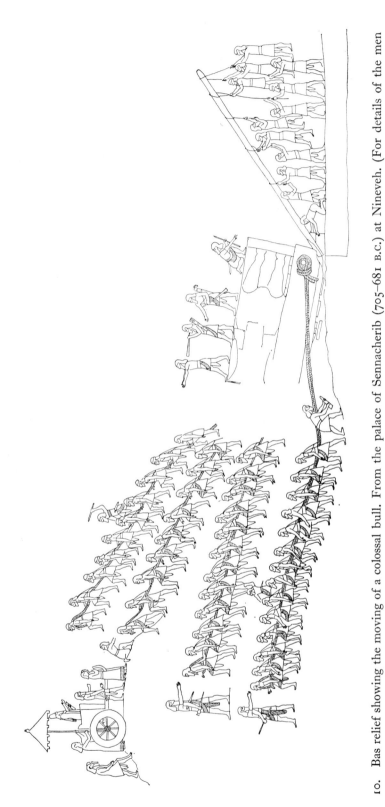

10. Bas relief showing the moving of a colossal bull. From the palace of Sennacherib (705–681 B.C.) at Nineveh. (For details of the men with trumpets see Pl. XVI). A. H. Layard, *Monuments of Nineveh* (London, 1853), pl. 15 (BM. 124820).

of them, a little over eight centimetres high, of cast bronze. Four still
have traces of the internal loop from which the clapper was suspended.
The others are smaller, between two and four centimetres high, and
there are two main types. In one, the bells are cone-shaped, with open
tops and figure-of-eight hanging loops (Pl. xxa). The iron clappers seem
to have been suspended from small bars placed across the top of the
opening and traces of both bars and tongues remain in some of the
bells. The other type is tubular, also with an open top, but with a single
hanging loop and a bar for the clapper inserted into holes in each side
of the body (Pl. xxb). A few are tubular but have a figure-of-eight hanging loop and there are several cone-shaped bells with closed tops and
single loops (Pl. xxc). There are also a number of tiny bells of very thin
bronze, cone-shaped, hemispherical or flattened hemispherical (Pl. xxd).
The function of all these bells is not known for certain. The tiny bells,
of which that shown in Pl. xixb is a charmingly decorated and well-
preserved example, may have been worn on ceremonial clothing, as we
know was done by Jewish high priests and early medieval Christian
clergy in Wales and Ireland.[42] This use was certainly magical in origin.
It is perhaps significant that the shapes of some of these Assyrian bells
are also those of some Indian bells. Even in the forms which are now
mass-produced for tourists, Indian temple bells, water-carriers' bells,
camel and elephant bells, bells of the Festival of Lights, give a range of
sounds which differ greatly according to the shape and nature and function of the bell. This range was probably as familiar in ancient Western
Asia as in present-day Eastern Asia, though it never became a significant
part of Western European musical experience in historic times. There is
also a certain resemblance between Assyrian bells and some of Celtic[43]
and Persian[44] provenance.

Little is known of the origins of bell-casting. It may have developed in
Asia or in the Caucasian region and spread westward during the second
millennium B.C. Pls. xviiic-d show a bell-rattle (of perforated bronze
with a bronze 'marble' inside) and an octagonal bell of about 1000 B.C.,
from Amlash in north-west Persia.

Small funnel-shaped *cymbals* which are clashed horizontally are
shown on one relief from the Palace of Sennacherib, and the fragments
in Pls. xxia, b seem to be remains of this kind of cymbal. Unlike the flat

42. [And see a stela of about the first century B.C. from Hierapolis in Syria showing
a priest with bells on his robe, H. Seyrig, *Syria* XX (1939), Pl. XXVI and pp. 183–188.]
43. J. Moreau, *Die Welt der Kelten* (Stuttgart, 1958), Pl. 46.
44. H. H. von der Osten, *Die Welt der Perser* (Stuttgart, 1956), Pl. 34.

variety shown in Pls. xxic, d, they have not survived to the present day, though cup-shaped cymbals are still played in eastern Asia.

The Assyrians enjoyed the products of foreign craftsmanship in objects given as tribute, taken in war, and acquired by normal trading or by the importation of foreign workmen. Phoenician ivory, carved, engraved, painted or inlaid was used in the decoration of furniture and for table and toilet ware, and it is on such pieces that we find the only portrayals of female musicians from Western Asia at this period other than the singers and dancers of the defeated Elamites which have come from Assyria. Fragments of a roughly incised panel show two figures, one with double pipes and one with a *rectangular lyre* possibly of Hurrian or Mitannian origin, which also appears once (played by a male musician) on an Ashurbanipal relief. On the fragments of a Phoenician or Syrian ivory pyxis (Pl. viib) found in the South-East Palace at Nimrud there are double pipes, tambour and two small *zithers*. The artist of this piece was faced with the same problem of presentation as the engraver of the procession on the bronze bowl from Iran in Pl. viia. The ivory carving has greater charm and movement as a whole, and the difficult zither-playing figure is deftly portrayed turning her head and shoulders full-front towards the viewer, so that her hands fit naturally at her instrument even though it is shown upright. It has been suggested that these instruments are not zithers but 'xylophones', comparable to the so-called 'Apulean sistrum'.[45]

There is no direct evidence about the function of the shaped, engraved and perforated shells which were found at Nimrud, Isfahan (Pl. xxii), Sippar and Tepe Giyan. The suggestion that they were *clappers* used by dancers[46] is reasonable. We know that the solo dancing girls of other ancient civilisations performed to the sound of their own finger-cymbals, clappers or small tambours, just as *flamenco* dancers do with castanets, and the lack of Western Asiatic counterparts of the many Egyptian, Indian and early Greek portrayals of 'show girls' is perhaps due to conventions of content in representation rather than to the absence of this kind of entertainment (see Figs. 11 and 12). It is possible that the slightly larger shells of near-circular cut (Pls. xxiib-c) were tied in pairs with pellets between them to form rattles rather than clappers. The rattle was not always and still is not in non-European societies the trivial soundmaker which it has become in the West.

45. Max Wegner, *Die Musikinstrumente des Alten Orients*, (Münster, 1950), p. 49.
46. R. D. Barnett, 'Hamath and Nimrud', *Iraq* 25 (1963), pp. 81–5.

11. Detail from a mosaic pavement showing a dancing girl with clappers. From Carthage, 4th century A.D. Height of figure 120 cm. (BM., Department of Greek and Roman Antiquities, No. 15).

12. Pair of bronze clappers on wooden arms and with a leather handle. From Egypt, about 400 A.D. Length 34 cm., (BM., Department of Egyptian Antiquities, 54014).

TERRACOTTAS OF THE HELLENISTIC PERIOD

Historians of art frequently give little attention and museum curators little display space to material from times in which civilisations are considered to have been in decline. The survival of prodigious quantities of Greek objects and the influence which the civilisation of Greece, in however misconstrued a form, has had on later European societies has tended to obliterate interest in older seats of civilisation like Mesopotamia and Egypt in the latter part of the first millennium. For anthropologists, sociologists and students of human behaviour in general, complex transition periods such as these can be immensely fascinating. The populations of Western Asia were by this time as mixed ethnically as those of the late Roman Empire or of the United States of America in the twentieth century. The Sumerian and Akkadian (Babylonian) languages were by then known only to scholars and scribes. Aramaic had replaced Akkadian as the common international language. The worship of Iranian gods came to Mesopotamia with the Persian officials of Darius and Xerxes. The Greek gods came with the founding of Greek-style cities by Greco-Macedonian colonists and with the reorganisation of existing cities on the Greek model.

41

Musical depictions which survive from this time show little Greek influence. It is probable that, for all the Greeks' complex theoretical writing about music, mostly by non-musicians, it was in fact the least original part of Greek civilisation and the least attractive to peoples who had older and more colourful musical traditions of their own.

Three kinds of *double pipes* are shown on the terracottas of the Hellenistic period in the Department of Western Asiatic Antiquities. Short, divergent pipes of equal length are played by a satyr, long divergent equal pipes by a draped figure, and in two groups of paired figures from Babylon (Pl. xxiiia) and Warka, one figure plays long divergent unequal pipes and the other a small basin-shaped drum. The worn condition of these figures makes it impossible to see details of players or instruments. In two pairs of similar figures from Nippur (now in the University Museum, Philadelphia) the musicians are clearly girls and the pipes are long and equal. Comparable instruments on well-preserved sculptures of the seventh and sixth centuries B.C. from Cyprus[47] and from Boğazköy[48] have long double reeds, like modern oboe and bassoon reeds in construction, but much larger. We do not know when or where this kind of reed, as distinct from the simpler, non-lip-controlled single reed, was evolved or created.

The *harps* are all vertical angled instruments, smaller than the big Assyrian vertical harps and of somewhat different form. There are two kinds. One has a sound-box of roughly the same depth throughout, set at a right angle to the string-carrying arm. (The earliest known depiction of this type appears to be from Egypt in the time of Amenophis II, 1450–1425 B.C.). There is an Egyptian specimen, probably of late date, in the Cairo Museum,[49] another in the Archaeological Museum in Florence, which seems to be an assemblage of the parts of two harps, as well as a number of reliefs and terracotta figures of players. This right-angled harp with vertical sound-box is generally considered to have been introduced into Egypt from Western Asia in the middle of the second millennium B.C. and it may be due only to the fortuitousness of survival that iconographical evidence from Mesopotamia comes from a much later time. Pl. xxiiib shows a pair of figures, found at Babylon, one of which holds a right-angled harp and the other a pair of small

47. F. N. Pryce, *Catalogue of Sculpture in the Dept. of Greek and Roman Antiquities of the British Museum*, Vol. I, pt. 2 (London, 1931), p. 26, Figs. 23–5.

48. E. Akurgal, *Die Kunst Anatoliens von Homer bis Alexander* (Berlin, 1961), Figs. 55 and 57.

49. H. Besseler and M. Schneider (eds.), *Musikgeschichte in Bildern* II. 1. H. Hickmann, *Ägypten* (Leipzig, 1961), Pl. 98.

cymbals. We know nothing of the religious or other associations of these figures but it may be worth noting that the pairs show one tune-playing and one percussion instrument. This was the combination in the music for the rites of Cybele, one religion of Asiatic origin about which we know something from later sources.

The other kind of vertical harp found on the terracottas is documented from Egypt to Persia. The figure shown in Pl. xxiva comes from Babylon. The sound-box is expanded in depth towards the top and it is set at an angle to the string-carrying arm, so that it frequently has a top-heavy appearance. This is the only vertical harp of antiquity in which the depth of the sound-box is related to the string lengths, i.e. enlarging gradually as the strings are increased in length. This acoustic refinement was present on some of the big arched harps of Egypt from the middle of the second millennium B.C. onwards, curiously coincident with the small vertical right-angled harp on which it was not present. The plectrum-plucked horizontal harps of Mesopotamia had this kind of box though the big vertical harps apparently did not.

Lyres appear on three terracottas. That played by the figure (perhaps intended to represent Apollo) in Pl. xxivb is of the round-based kind which, like the lute, may have been introduced into Mesopotamia by mountain people from Iran early in the second millennium B.C. Round-based lyres in various forms were the characteristic stringed instruments of the early Cretan and Aegean civilisations and a great number of depictions of them survives. The old Greek *phorminx*, Homer's lyre, was of this type. The phorminx, however, does not appear in Greek iconography after the seventh century B.C., nor is its more elaborate form, the long-armed phorminx, shown after the middle of the fifth century B.C. There is a round-based lyre on a relief from Warka of the middle of the second millennium and many from Western Anatolia, Cyprus and Crete (sometimes on work of Syrian provenance) from the ninth century B.C. onwards. The same lyre as that in Pl. xxivb appears on another terracotta where it is played by an ape. In this piece the fan-shaped stringing which seems to have been characteristic of the later round-based lyres can be seen[50]. The third lyre, held by a robed figure whose head is missing, is on a terracotta from Warka. It is a long rectangular lyre which also may have come into Mesopotamia originally from Iran during the second millennium B.C. It appears on reliefs from Anatolia[51]

50. A hollow cast bronze figurine of the early first millennium A.D. from South Arabia shows, not very distinctly, a seated woman playing a similar round-based lyre (Pl. xxva).

51. H. T. Bossert, *Altanatolien* (Berlin, 1942), Nos. 810 and 949.

and, held semi-horizontally and played with a plectrum, on some Assyrian reliefs, on a silver bowl from Cyprus[52] and on the incised ivory fragment mentioned on page 40.

To the twentieth-century European mind, the small winged figure playing *panpipes* (Pl. xxvb) has Greek associations. It is unlikely that it had such associations in Western Asia. It is true that no known fragments which survive from neolithic sites can be identified as components of panpipes as certainly as some can be identified as whistles and rim-blown and plugged flutes; but the distribution of panpipes among primitive agricultural peoples over a wide area in Melanesia, South America, Europe and Asia suggests an origin at the latest in a neolithic stage, which in Western Asia was pre-Hellenic by many millennia.

We know nothing of the significance of these musician figures but it is likely that they had religious or cult associations. In Greek legend, the place of origin of panpipes and of the auletic arts was said to have been Phrygia. Players of double pipes and lyre flank the splendid Phrygian figure of the Mother Goddess, of the sixth century B.C., now at Ankara, which was found at Boğazköy,[53] and double pipes, small tambour and cymbals were the ritual instruments in the worship of Cybele which reached Rome from Asia Minor in the second century B.C. In connection with the Cybelean pipes, which had an upturned bell at the end of the long drone pipe and were known to the Roman world as the Phrygian aulos, it is worth remembering the little eighth century B.C. bronze figure in a Phrygian cap, playing a hornpipe, and the dark woman hornpiper on the Cretan sarcophagus of six centuries earlier still.

Our knowledge of music in ancient societies in which it was essentially an aurally-transmitted art can never be more than sketchy. The fortuitousness of the survival of objects, and conventions, of which we are ignorant, as to what musical subjects could be depicted in those societies, inevitably make it unbalanced as well as sketchy. But however imperfect our knowledge of ancient Western Asiatic music, some of its instrumental legacies are still with us in the twentieth century. Some are distant and tenuous survivals; some are part of ancient but vigorous regional musical traditions; some, like the European harp, the lute, the guitar and the violin and clarinet families, are evolved or mechanised forms whose earliest prototypes were ancient Western Asiatic.

52. E. Gjerstad, *Opuscula Archaeologica*, IV, Pl. xvi.
53. Akurgal, *Kunst Anatoliens*, Fig. 55.

APPENDIX I

Musical Instruments and Monuments representing Musical Instruments in the Department of Western Asiatic Antiquities

STRING INSTRUMENTS

Harps

Actual
  Early Dynastic period: 121198 (Fig. 2)
Represented
  Old Babylonian period, terracottas: 23715; 127478 (Pl. va)
  Assyrian period, reliefs:
    Ashurnasirpal II: 124533; 124535; 124548; 124550 (Pl. IX); (bronze) 124690
    Shalmaneser III: (bronze) 124662
    Sennacherib: 124848
    Ashurbanipal: 118916 (Pl. xv and Fig. 8); 124802 (Pls. XIII–XIV); 124886; 124920; (Pl. x); 124922 (Pl. XII)
  Hellenistic period, terracottas: 91794, (Pl. xxIIIb); 91808 (Pl. xxIva); 91816; 91859; 116659; 118947; 127336; 127337; 80-11-12, 1920; 81-4-28, 950, 960

Lyres

Actual
  Early Dynastic period: 121199 (Pl. II); 121198 (Fig. 3)
Represented
  Early Dynastic period: 121201 (*Frontispiece*)
  Late second millennium B.C., seal: 134306 (Pl. vIIIa and Fig. 6)
  Assyrian period, reliefs:
    Sennacherib: 124947 (Pl. XI)
    Ashurbanipal: 118916 (Pl. xv and Fig. 8); 124922 (Pl. XII)
  Assyrian period, seal: 89359
  Hellenistic period, terracottas: 91796; 91813; 91817 (Pl. xxIvb)
  Early first millennium A.D., South Arabia, 122020 (Pl. xxva)

Lutes

Represented
  Akkadian period, seals: 28806; 89096 (Pl. Ivc)
  Old Babylonian period, terracottas; 91889; 108843 (Pl. Iva); 118001 (Pl. Ivb); 53-12-19, 46
  Assyrian period, relief:
    Ashurnasirpal II: 124548
  Hellenistic period, terracotta: 23656

45

Zithers

Represented

Early second millennium B.C., Persia: 128620 (Pl. vIIb and Fig. 5)

Assyrian period, ivory: 118179 (Pl. vIIa)

WIND INSTRUMENTS

Trumpet

Represented

Early first millennium B.C., Caria: 130909 (Pl. vIIIb)

Assyrian period, reliefs:

Sennacherib: 124820 (Pl. xvi and Fig. 10); 124823

Vertical Flute

Represented

Akkadian period, seal: 102417

Hornpipes

Represented

Early first millennium B.C.: 134975 (Pl. vIIIc)

Double Pipes

Represented

Assyrian period, reliefs:

Ashurbanipal: 124802 (Pl. xIII); 124922 (Pl. xII)

Assyrian period, ivories: 118179 (Pl. vIIa); 127094

Hellenistic period, terracottas: 23656; 91807 (Pl. xxIIIa); 91820; 91892; 117709; 127339; 80-11-12, 1897

Pan Pipes

Represented

Hellenistic period, terracotta: 88-5-12, 742 (Pl. xxvb)

Whistle

Actual

Ninth-eighth century B.C., Persia, terracotta: 134950 (Pl. vIIId)

PERCUSSION INSTRUMENTS

Drums

Represented

Old Babylonian period, terracotta: 91906 (Pl. vb)

Assyrian period, reliefs:

Ashurbanipal: 124802, (Pl. xIII); 124920 (Pl. x)

Hellenistic period, terracottas: 91807 (Pl. xxIIIa); 91892

46

Friction Drum

Represented

First millennium B.C., terracotta: 80-11-12, 1923 (Pl. vid)

Tambours

Represented

Old Babylonian period, terracottas: 103369 (Pl. vic); 116800; 117131; 123234 (Pl. via); 127338 (Pl. vib); 1931-10-10, 417, 429, 439; 1933-10-13, 200

Early second millennium B.C., Persia: 128620 (Pl. viib and Fig. 5)

Assyrian period, reliefs:

Ashurnasirpal II: 124550 (Pl. ix)

Sennacherib: 124948

Assyrian period, ivories: 118179 (Pl. viia); 126515

Hellenistic period, terracotta: 81-4-28, 946

Cymbals

Actual

Assyrian period, bronze: 91388 (Pl. xxic); N.108; N.114; N.115; N.116 (Pl. xxia); N.512 (Pl. xxid); N.558 (Pl. xxib); N.559–569; N.574; N.1835; N.1838; 83-1-18, 668

Seventh century B.C., Persia: 134911, 134941

Represented

Old Babylonian period, terracotta: 91906 (Pl. vb)

Assyrian period, reliefs:

Sennacherib: 124948

Hellenistic period, terracotta: 91794 (Pl. xxiiib)

Clappers

Actual

First millennium B.C., shell

Assyria: 124603; 124605; 124606; 133008 (Pl. xxiic); 133009; 133010; 133011; 133012 (Pl. xxiia); 134325 (Pl. xxiia)

Babylonia: 82-9-18A, 28

Persia: 128654; 128870 (Pl. xxiib)

Bells

Actual

Early first millennium B.C., Persia: 134703 (Pl. xixd)

Assyrian period: 48353; 91366; 91368; 98934; 98935 (Pl. xxc); 98936 (Pl. xxd); 127341 (Pl. xxd); N.155–158; N.159 (Pl. xixa); N.160–161; N.162 (Pl. xxb); N.163; N.164 (Pl. xxa); N.165–183; N.184 (Pl. xxa); N.185–187; N.188 (Pl. xxa); N.189–204; N.205 (Pl. xxb); N.206–228; N.1836, N.1837; 55-12-5, 272, 297; 80-7-19, 254-255; 81-7-1, 3385 (Pl. xixb); 81-11-3, 1957 (Pl. xxc); 82-5-22, 334 (Pl. xxd); 83-1-18, 668; 1929-10-12, 262 (Pl. xxd); 1930-5-8, 128, 129 (Pl. xxd); 130 (Pl. xxd), 131

47

Represented
Assyrian period, reliefs:
Tiglath-pileser III: 118905 (Pl. XVII)
Sennacherib: 12477; 124780; 124902; 124903; 124913
Ashurbanipal: 124793; 124801; 124805; 124807; 124809; 124853;
    124856; 124857; 124859; 124867; 124869; 124874; 124875;
    124876 (Pl. XVIII); 124929; 124939

Bell Rattle

Actual
Early first millennium B.C., Persia; 134704 (Pl. XIXc)

Rattles

Actual
Animal form: 92015; 105060; 116706 (Pl. IIIa); 116860; 116865
    (Pl. IIIa); 116866 (Pl. IIIa); 124481 (Pl. IIIa); 128656 (Pl. IIIa);
    1931-10-10, 499 (Pl. IIIa); 507
Bird form: 166867; 119148; 127469 (Pl. IIIa); 127730; 1931-10-10, 486
'Pie crust' type: 116529; 116868; 116869; 120082; 122050; 1919-11-11,
    1781; 1927-5-27, 249 (Pl. IIIb); 1931-10-10, 508
Others: 115887; 120904

GENERAL BIBLIOGRAPHY

BIGGS, R. D. 'The Sumerian Harp', *The American Harp Journal,* I, 3 (New
    York, 1968), pp. 6–12.
FARMER, H. G. 'The Music of Ancient Mesopotamia' in WELLESZ, E. (ed.),
    Ancient and Oriental Music (New Oxford History of Music, I), (London,
    1957), pp. 228–254.
GALPIN, F. W. *The Music of the Sumerians, Babylonians and Assyrians* (Cam-
    bridge, 1937) [now in need of drastic revision and correction].
HARTMANN, H. *Die Musik der sumerischen Kultur* (Frankfurt am Main, 1960).
KRAELING, C. H. and MOWRY, L. 'Music in the Bible' in WELLESZ, *op. cit.,*
    pp. 283–312. See under FARMER above.
PARROT, A. 'Mesopotamian Music' in *Nineveh and Babylon* (London, 1961),
    pp. 296–312.
PRITCHARD, J. B. *The Ancient Near East in Pictures Relating to the Old
    Testament* (Princeton, 1954), Nos 191–205.
SACHS, C. *The History of Musical Instruments* (New York, 1940), pp. 67–85
    (Sumer and Babylonia), 105–127 (Israel) [now in need of revision].
STAUDER, W. *Die Harfen und Leiern der Sumerer* (Frankfurt am Main, 1957).
STAUDER, W. *Die Harfen und Leiern Vorderasiens in babylonischer und assy-
    rischer Zeit* (Frankfurt am Main, 1961).
WEGNER, M. *Die Musikinstrumente des Alten Orients* (Münster, 1950).
WOOLLEY, C. L. *Ur Excavations* II, *The Royal Cemetery* (London & Phila-
    delphia, 1934), pp. 249–261.

APPENDIX II

Music in the Old Testament

MUSICIANS

Musicians and music, both secular (1 Ki.IV.32, this and the following references are typical, not exhaustive) and religious (Ps.CL.3-5) are mentioned frequently in the Old Testament. Among words used in this connection, which give some idea of the range of music, are the verb *nāgan*, 'to play a stringed instrument' (1 Sam.XVI.23) and the related forms *nōgēn*, 'player' (Ps.LXXXVII.25) and *něgînâ* (plural *něgînôth*)', music of a stringed instrument(?)', which occurs in several Psalm headings. More specific are the verbs *tāphaph*, 'to play the tambour (*tōph*)' (Ps.LXVIII.25), and *ḥālal*, 'to play the double pipe (*ḥālîl*)' (Ps.LXXXVII.7). The term 'chief musician', which occurs in the headings of many of the Psalms, is a participle, *měnaṣṣēăḥ*, meaning literally 'overseer', and may have signified something like 'director of music' or 'choirmaster'.

MUSICAL INSTRUMENTS IN ISRAEL

The identifications of all the instruments mentioned in the Old Testament are in varying degrees uncertain. In the accompanying chart those with a question mark are particularly uncertain. That instruments were used in combinations is shown by 1 Sam.X.5 (harp, tambour, double pipe and lyre), 2 Sam.VI.5 (lyres, harps, tambours, rattles and cymbals), 1 Chr.XXV.1 (lyres, harps and cymbals), and 1 Chr.XV.16–28, where the bringing of the ark to Jerusalem by David is said to have been accompanied by singing and shouting, and the playing of harps, lyres, horns, trumpets and cymbals.

BABYLONIAN INSTRUMENTS

In Daniel III the Babylonian instrumental group of Nebuchadnezzar is described. The possible, though in several cases uncertain, identifications of the instruments are given in the second part of the accompanying chart.

THE MUSIC PLAYED

No precise information about scales, melodies or harmony has survived. Some hints about rhythms may be derived from the accent marks which accompany the consonantal text of the Hebrew Bible, and it may be that these same accents indicated changes of pitch, but the details of this are not now known. Moreover the text was only provided with accents by the Jewish scholars known as Masoretes during the first millenium A.D., several centuries after its original composition, so there is no guarantee that they represent the situation in ancient Israel.

1 Instrument	2 Hebrew Name	3 Rendering in Authorised Version	4 Passages where Renderings in column 3 Occur	5 Comments
ISRAELITE				
String Instruments				
Harp	nēbel	psaltery viol	passim Is.v.12; XIV.11; Amos v.23; VI.5.	A 'ten stringed harp', or possibly 'harp <and> zither'(?)
	nēbel 'āśôr	psaltery *and* an instrument of ten strings.	Ps.XXX.2; CXLIV.9.	
Lyre Zither(?)	kinnôr 'āśôr	harp instrument of ten strings	passim Ps.XCII.4.	Literally 'a ten'.
Wind Instruments				
Horn	shōphār	trumpet cornet	passim	An animal's horn.
	qeren hay-yôbēl yôbēl ḥăṣōṣĕrâ	ram's horn trumpet trumpet	1 Chr.XV.28; 2 Chr.XV.14; Ps.XCVIII.6; Hos.V.8. Jos.VI.5. Ex.XIX.13. passim	An animal's horn. An animal's horn. Sometimes of silver, Nu.X.2.
Trumpet	(?) tāqôă'	trumpet	Ezek VII.14.	A wind instrument for summoning to battle.
Vertical flute(?)	'ûgāb	organ	Gn.IV.21; Job.XXI.12; XXX.31; Ps.CL.4.	Cf. the verb ḥālal, Ps. LXXXVII.7.
Double pipe(?)	ḥālîl	pipe	passim	
Percussion Instruments				
Tambour	tôph	timbrel	passim	Cf. the verb tāphaph,

Bell	pa'ămōn	bell	Ex.xxviii.33,34; xxxix.25, 26.	See p. 39 and n. 42.
Sistrum(?)	měṣillā	bell	Zech.xiv.20.	
	měna'anĕă'	cornet	2 Sam.vi.5.	or rattle(?)
BABYLONIAN	*Aramaic Name*			
String Instruments				
Horizontal harp(?)	śabk	sackbut	Dan.iii	
Vertical harp(?)	pěsanterîn	psaltery	Dan.iii	
Lyre	qaytěrōs	harp	Dan.iii	
Wind Instruments				
Horn	qeren	cornet	Dan.iii	
Double pipe(?)	mashrōqî	flute	Dan.iii	
Percussion Instruments(??)				
Drum(??)	sûmpōnĕyâ	dulcimer	Dan.iii	Or perhaps not an instrument but a summary of the others, 'full consort'.

...w of the 'Great Death Pit' (Grave 1237) at Ur, during excavation, showing three lyres ...he ground. These are now, from left to right, in London (B.M. 121199; see plate II), ...adelphia and Baghdad.

Silver lyre (B.M. 121199) as initially reconstructed by the excavator (see cove
From Ur, about 2600 B.C.
Height 106cm.

Terracotta rattles in the form of animals (B.M. 127469; 116706; 116866; 116865; 1931-10-10, 499; 124481; 128656)
128656 from Tepe Giyan, remainder from Babylonia, early second millennium B.C.
Height of bird 10·1 cm.

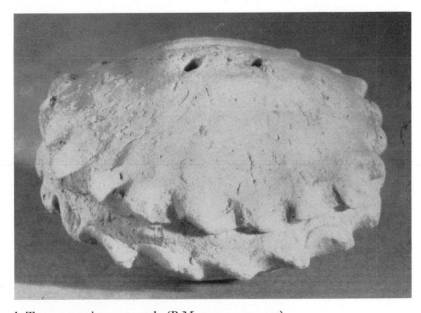

b Terracotta pie-crust rattle (B.M. 1927-5-27, 249).
From Ur, early second millennium B.C.
Diameter 7 cm.

a

b

a Terracotta plaque showing kilted lute player
(B.M. 108843).
From Babylonia, early second millennium B.C.
Height 7·5 cm.

b Terracotta figurine of nude lute player
(B.M. 118001).
From Babylonia, early second millennium B.C.
Height 8·2 cm.

c Impression of cylinder seal showing a birdman
being brought before a seated god (B.M.
89096) and detail of bottom left, showing seated
lute player.
Akkadian period, about 24th century B.C.
Height 3·8 cm.

a

a Terracotta plaque showing a seated female
  harpist (B.M. 127478).
  From Ur, early second millennium B.C.
  Height 9 cm.
b Terracotta plaque showing wrestling figures
  with drummer and cymbal player
  (B.M. 91906).
  From Larsa, early second millennium B.C.
  Height 7 cm.

b

a Terracotta figurine of nude woman with
  tambour(?) (B.M. 123234).
  From Ur, early second millennium B.C.
  Height 13·3 cm.
b Terracotta figurine of woman with
  tambour(?) (B.M. 127338).
  From Ur, early second millennium B.C.
  Height 5·7 cm.
c Terracotta plaque showing draped figure
  with tambour(?) (B.M. 103369).
  Second millennium B.C.
  Height 6·9 cm.
d Terracotta figurine of a monkey with a
  friction-drum(?) (B.M. 80-11-12, 1923).
  From Babylon, 7th–6th century B.C.
  Height 6 cm.

Fragment of Phoenician
or Syrian ivory pyxis
showing musicians with
kithers, tambour and
double pipes in procession
towards a goddess
(B.M. 118179).
From Nimrud, 8th
century B.C.
Height 6·7 cm.

Fragment of bronze situla showing procession of musicians (B.M. 128620)
From Tepe Giyan, west Persia, early second millennium B.C.
Height 9 cm. See Fig. 5.

a Cylinder seal and impression showing a lyre
player and files of birds and animals
(B.M. 134306).
From Mardin, Turkey, *c.* 1200 B.C.
Height 2·2 cm.
See Fig. 6.

b Bronze figurine of a trumpeter
(B.M. 130909).
From Caria, about 800 B.C.
Height 6 cm.

c Bronze figurine of a man wearing a
scalloped tunic and Phrygian cap, playing
a hornpipe (B.M. 134975)
From Asia Minor
Height 7·6 cm.
d Clay whistle in the form of a seated figure
(B.M. 134950).
From Iran, about 800 B.C.
Height 8·4 cm.

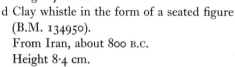

Detail from relief of Ashurnasirpal II (883–859 B.C.) showing horizontal harps and small tambour. From Nimrud (B.M. 124550).

X

Relief of Ashurbanipal (668–626 B.C.) showing long drum and vertical harp. From Nineveh. Height 58 cm. (B.M. 124920).

lief of Sennacherib (705–681 B.C.) showing three lyre players (B.M. 124947).
om Nineveh.
eight 99 cm.

Detail from relief of Ashurbanipal showing double pipes, vertical harp, and lyre (B.M. 124922).
From Nineveh.

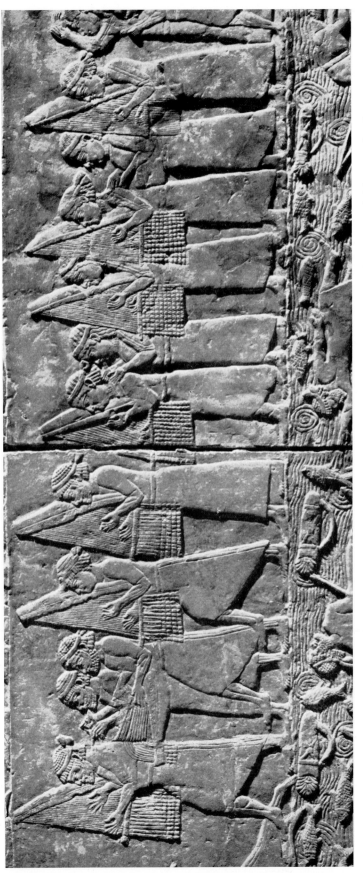

XIII

Detail from relief of Ashurbanipal showing Elamite musicians (B.M. 124802). From Nineveh. Continuation of this scene in plate XIVa.

b

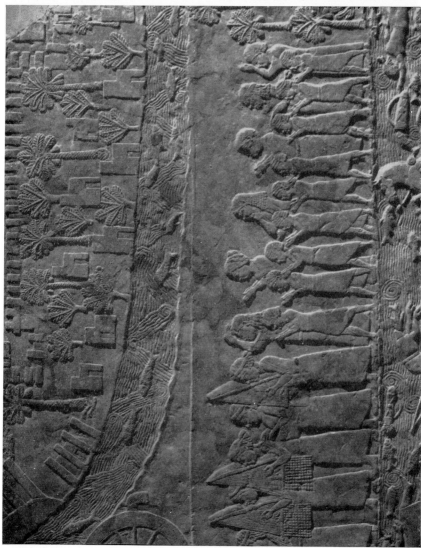

a

Details from relief of Ashurbanipal showing Elamite musicians (B.M. 124802). From Nineveh.

elief of Ashurbanipal (668–626 B.C.) showing a lyre player and a harpist walking with a
med lion among trees (B.M. 118916). From Nineveh.
eight 168 cm.   For detail of lyre player, see Fig. 8.

Detail from relief of Sennacherib showing two figures with trumpets (B.M. 124820). From Nineveh.

For complete scene see Fig. 10.

Detail from relief of Tiglath-pileser III (745–727 B.C.) showing a horse's head with a bell (B.M. 118905).
From Nimrud.

a Bronze horse bell (B.M. N.159).
  From Nimrud, 9th–8th century B.C.
  Height 8·2 cm.
b Miniature bronze bell (B.M. 81-7-1,
  3385).
  From Assyria, 9th–8th century B.C.
  Height 2·8 cm.

c Bronze bell-rattle (B.M. 134704)
  From Amlash, north-west Persia, about
  1000 B.C.
  Height 10·3 cm.
d Octagonal bronze bell (B.M. 134703)
  From Amlash, north-west Persia, about 1000 B.C.
  Height 12·1 cm.

a

b

c

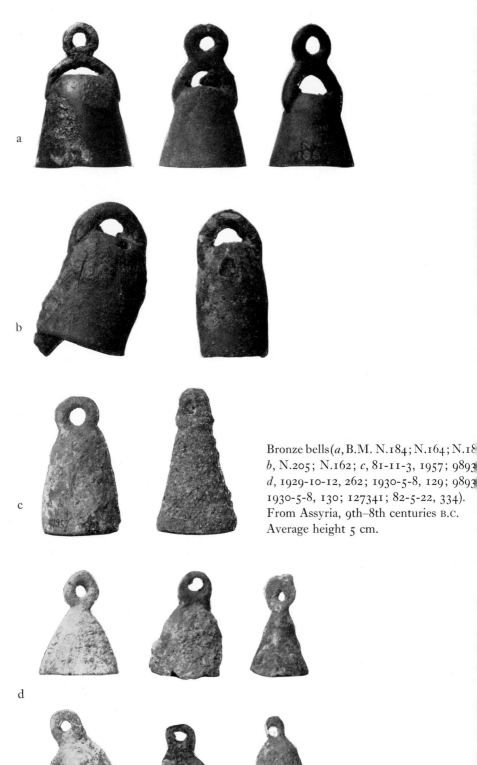

Bronze bells (a, B.M. N.184; N.164; N.18
b, N.205; N.162; c, 81-11-3, 1957; 9893
d, 1929-10-12, 262; 1930-5-8, 129; 9893
1930-5-8, 130; 127341; 82-5-22, 334).
From Assyria, 9th–8th centuries B.C.
Average height 5 cm.

d

Bronze cymbals (B.M. N.116, N.558, 91388, N.512).
From Nimrud, 9th–8th centuries B.C.
Diameter of a. 6·3 cm.

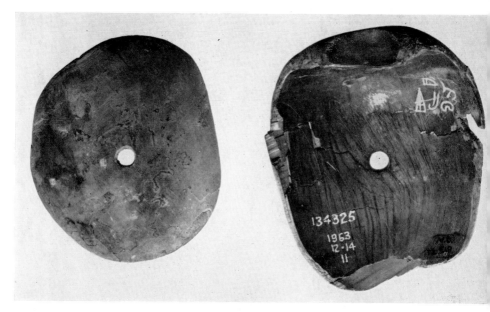

a

Shell clappers
a From Nimrud, 9th century B.C. (B.M. 133012, 134325). Diameters 5·8 and 6·5 cm.
b From Isfahan (B.M. 128870). Diameter 10 cm.
c From Nimrud (B.M. 133008). Diameter 9·9 cm.

b   c

a Terracotta double figurine with double pipes
and drum (B.M. 91807).
From Babylon, late first millennium B.C.
Height 13·2 cm.

Terracotta double figurine
with vertical harp and cymbals
(B.M. 91794).
From Babylon, late first
millennium B.C.
Height 16·8 cm.

a Terracotta figurine of a woman with
a vertical harp (B.M. 91808).
From Babylon, late first millennium B.C.
Height 16·8 cm.

b Terracotta figurine of a man with a
lyre (B.M. 91817).
Late first millennium B.C.
Height 12·8 cm.

a Bronze statuette of a woman with a lyre (B.M. 122020). From South Arabia, early first millennium A.D. Height 6·4 cm.

b Terracotta figurine of a winged figure playing panpipes (B.M. 88-5-12, 742). Late first millennium B.C. Height 11·3 cm.